CLASSIC REVIVAL

Spanish c. 1780

American c. 1790

English "Carlton House" desk c. 1780

French "semanier" c. 1760

French "lit a la polonaise" c. 1785

Danish c. 1780

NEO-CLASSIC

German c. 1820

American c. 1810

English c. 1810

French "méridienne" c. 1796

Austrian c. 1810

ABOUT THE COVER: *Part of a set long known as "the furniture of the Gods," this armchair was ordered about 1770 for Mme. du Barry, last mistress of Louis XV. In style, the chair is transitional. The curves of the Louis XV mode are less extreme, and the carving anticipates classic revival elements of the Louis XVI style.*

ACKNOWLEDGMENTS: *Cleveland Museum of Art, Gift of Hanna Fund:* det. from The Music Party *by Pieter de Hooch, 8. Fundamental Photographs: 38; from Henry Moses' Designs of Modern Costume, 1823, 41. G. P. Putnam's Sons, reprinted by permission from* Great Palaces of Europe *with an introduction by Sacheverell Sitwell,* © 1964 *by Weidenfeld & Nicolson, Ltd.: 37. Henry Francis du Pont Winterthur Museum: 11, 12, 17 left, 24, 32, 42. Musée du Louvre: cover;* Le Déjeuner *by François Boucher, 18. Metropolitan Museum of Art: Dick Fund, 1935: det. from Duquevauviller engraving after Lavreince,* Assemblée au Salon, 26; *Fletcher Fund, 1934: 34 right; Kennedy Fund, 1918: 33; Gift of C. Ruxton Love, 1959: 35 right; Gift of J. Pierpont Morgan, 1906: 34 left; Rogers Fund, 1920, 1922, 1923: 23 left, 19 right, 35 left; Gift of Samuel H. Kress Foundation, 1958: 27; Gifts of Irwin Untermyer, 1955, 1956: 16 right, 30; Irwin Untermyer Collection: 13, 23 right; 20, 29, 31. National Gallery of Art, Washington, D.C., Samuel H. Kress Collection:* Napoleon *by Jacques-Louis David, 38. Philadelphia Museum of Art, McFadden Collection:* det. from The Assembly at Wanstead House *by William Hogarth, 15. Réalités photo* Connaissance des Arts *(Boitier) Col. particulière: 16 left. Stitching Johan Maurits Huis Van Nassau: det. from* Jacob Feitama and His Wife *by Wybrand Hendriks, 28. Trustees of the Wallace Collection, London, photo by John R. Freeman & Co., Ltd.: 16; 17 right. Musée de Versailles, Cabinet de Louis XV: 19 left.*

GREAT FURNITURE STYLES

1660–1830

BY DONALD D. MACMILLAN

ILLUSTRATED BY PETER SPIER

THE ODYSSEY PRESS · NEW YORK

BECAUSE OF ITS peculiarly intimate association with basic human needs, furniture reflects the social history of an age. It is the machinery for living which men of every era have made either a simple necessity or a work of art, according to their own taste or culture. ■ George Hepplewhite, in his *Cabinet-Maker and Upholsterer's Guide* of 1788, proclaimed the common-sense approach to furniture design: "To unite elegance and utility, and blend the useful with the

Detail from Louis XIV and His Heirs *by N. de Largillière, 1710. The decoration of the room shows the lightening of detail which culminated in the rococo style. All the heirs were to die within two years, and the king in five.*

agreeable." But common sense has not always prevailed; less than a century before, Louis XIV took quite a different approach. In 1682 the Sun King installed his court at Versailles, a palace planned to be a tangible representation of his power. A state-sponsored group of the best designers and craftsmen of France worked unceasingly "to diffuse and uphold His Majesty's glory." ■ A setting of unparalleled magnificence called for furniture of equal magnificence. Exotic woods such as ebony, inlays of metal on tortoise shell, table tops of semi-precious stones, rare marbles, the finest lacquers of the Far East —all were combined with the most sumptuous gilded bronze mounts to enrich a relatively small number of furniture forms. ■ "This sort

Louis XIV c. 1680

Louis XIV c. 1680

Boulle commode c. 1700

In Holland the absence of a royal court produced a new type of patro[n], the capitalist. Trade with the Far East and the West Indies rapid[ly] made this tiny nation the richest in 17th century Europe. A prospero[us] middle class demanded the best cabinetwork, such as that shown in t[he] painting at LEFT. In England "new" pieces included wall mirrors, boo[k] cases, chests of drawers, clock cases, caned chairs, and dining table[s]

Dutch kast c. 1685

American c. 1715

Charles II c. 1660

Charles II c. 1670

Charles II c. 1660

Boulle bureau plat c. 1700

How to Recognize Baroque. *Motifs common to furniture of all countries were: Curved and distorted forms; heavy moldings and strong contrasts of light and shade; C and S scrolls; rich ornamentation; solid shell motifs and cartouches; twisted columns; contorted caryatids. The style derived from 17th century Roman architecture.*

of royal beauty," declared Mme. de Sévigné, "is unique in all the world." And unique it was in more ways than one, including its almost total disregard for human comfort. It may have upheld Louis' glory, but it did little to uphold human flesh and bone. At Louis' court, where some 10,000 status-seeking resident courtiers led a highly regimented life, furniture was a symbol, and the etiquette of seating became an obsession. There were armchairs for the royal family, side chairs for princes of the blood, stools for duchesses, and hassocks for ladies-in-waiting. Men almost always stood, except at cards; women sat only by permission. ■ Meanwhile, in 1660, Louis' royal cousin, Charles II, had arrived in England after a long exile enforced by the regicide of Charles I and the austere rule of Cromwell. He brought with him a cosmopolitan court whose members had become thoroughly familiar with French, Italian, and Dutch fashions. They had learned to admire all sorts of new materials and forms, and the Restoration marked the beginning of modern furniture styles in England. ■ Two cataclysmic events dealt the final blow to British furniture's "Age of Oak." The first was the Great Fire of London, which opened

9

the way for new architecture, interiors and furnishings. The second was Louis XIV's revocation of the Edict of Nantes; it sent thousands of the finest French craftsmen into exile, and many of them settled in England. ■ With the accession of William and Mary, who were called to England from Holland in 1687, the already close ties between the two countries became even closer, and soon their furniture designs were almost indistinguishable. Under the new rulers, form and the color and grain of wood assumed greater importance than intricate carving, which had been the passion of the two preceding courts, and the "Age of Walnut" reached its height. Walnut was used as a veneer on simple pieces, or was elaborately combined with exotic colored woods and other materials as marquetry. Pure curves served to balance a complexity of pattern which sometimes bordered on the ostentatious. ■ Dutch-influenced furniture design was enriched by a Huguenot refugee, Daniel Marot, who became court architect and designer. The growing trade with the Far East also brought in new ideas, including the motif of a dragon claw holding a pearl, which is believed to have led to the familiar and widely used claw-and-ball foot.

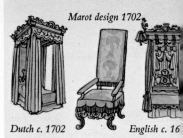

Marot design 1702

Dutch c. 1702   *English c. 16*

The cabriole (or curved) leg gradual supplanted straight, turned supports. T high chest of drawers on legs, later call a highboy, supplied storage for cloth

American butterfly table c. 1700

New England highboy c. 1

English gate-leg card table c. 1695

English cabinet on stand c. 1695

Trumpet turning

d linens. Tall-back chairs and sofas were completely padded
more luxurious comfort, and were often covered in fine
dlework, reflecting the English queen's hobby. Beds were
er to suit larger rooms, loftier ceilings, and a taste for dignity.

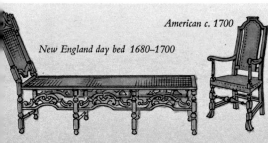

New England day bed 1680–1700

American c. 1700

In the American colonies, the William and Mary style appeared after a lag of some 15 years, and ran concurrently with the older Carolean and Jacobean forms. All were simplified to suit the scale of comparatively modest interiors and the taste of a society in a country that was still mainly wilderness. In this room, built in Virginia about 1715, familiar baroque elements, such as twisted columns, appear in the legs of the center table.

Spanish c. 1730

Dutch c. 1730

American c. 1730

The Queen Anne style, with its bold, pu
outlines and subtly rhythmic curves, is som
times reminiscent of Chinese furniture a
porcelain forms. Much of its internation
appeal lay in its adaptability to purely lo
idioms of ornament and materials.

Dutch 1730

In colonial America, the Queen Anne style, established in the 1730's, persisted into the 1750's to merge with the new "Chippendale" vogue. Men of wealth—shipowners and merchants of the North; planters of tobacco, rice and indigo in the South—enjoyed a steadily increasing trade with England and the West Indies. London was the center of culture, but a sturdy new society developed purely indigenous variations of well-known basic English forms.

American Philadelphia sofa c. 1740–50

■ Queen Anne's reign saw the rise of a style that took her name, although few monarchs were less interested in the arts. Carrying further the developments that had begun during the time of William and Mary, it moved away from the rectangular and heavy designs of earlier styles and toward curves and lightness. Anne's reign was short, but the style persisted and was for many years enormously popular in Holland, Spain, Italy, Portugal (and her colony, Brazil) and especially in the British colonies. It relied on beautiful woods and simple contours for its effect, and for that reason it found great favor with buyers of modest means. The emphasis was on quiet dignity, with no special tricks of turning or carving. "Queen Anne" furniture was lower and smaller in scale than that of previous styles, and it was markedly more comfortable. ■ As social life came more and more under the control of women, special pieces were created for them. Among such pieces were the desk and secretary, for writing social notes; the tea table, around which they gathered for polite conversation and scurrilous gossip; and the card table, at which they indulged their passion for games of chance. ■ None of Anne's 17 children

LEFT: *English card table, c. 1725, with needlework playing surface.*

13

England c. 1720   *William Kent c. 1726*   *George I c. 1720*

Americans of increasing means and sophistication were demanding furniture models which approximated a universally accepted standard of excellence. Advertisements began to appear announcing the establishments of craftsmen "newly arrived from London," or "trained in the latest mode."

American c. 1760   *American c. 1760*   *Dutch c. 1748*

survived her, and in 1714 the crown passed to a distant relative, George, Elector of Hanover. During his reign and that of the George who succeeded him, a series of able prime ministers maintained a comparative peace and prosperity which created an ideal climate for the growth of an immensely wealthy leisure class. The London court was dull, and old landed aristocrats and new moneyed capitalists set up little courts of their own on their vast country estates. ■ It was the age of the amateur architect, bursting with ideas gathered in Italy while on his obligatory "Grand Tour." Most notable was Lord Burlington, who popularized the designs by Palladio, the 16th century Italian architect, for "Roman" villas outside Venice. The Palladian style shaped architecture and interior design in England and America for two generations. ■ Meanwhile, French and continental patrons were beginning to favor refinement, elegance,

English gilded settee c. 1720   *Torchere c. 1730*

William Kent, Britain's first architect-decorator, captured the top patronage of the Palladian period. Like Le Brun at Versailles, he regarded each room as a separate work of art for which furniture must be specially designed. With more than a passing nod to the ornate baroque furniture of contemporary Rome and the great Venetian palazzos, he created a small repertory of architectural furniture forms, such as those shown in the Hogarth painting at RIGHT. At the same time, other furniture was designed for men of wealth who lived in houses, rather than palaces. A more ornate and more developed form of "Queen Anne," it was weightier and more vigorous of outline, often with carved grotesque ornaments.

ABOVE: *An American walnut lowboy combines elements of the William and Mary style—brush or "Spanish" feet—with Queen Anne features, such as a shaped skirt employing reverse curves.*

ABOVE RIGHT: *The undulating outlines and narrow verticality of this walnut easy chair are typical features of the Queen Anne style. English, c 1695.* LEFT: *André–Charles Boulle executed this extraordinary rich cabinet, a gift in 1700 from Louis XIV to his grandson, Philip V of Spain whose portrait appears on the center panel. Scenes of military life in tin, copper, ivory and mother of pearl are inlaid in red tortoise shell*

ABOVE: *A masterpiece of furniture designed in the French rococo manner, this chest of drawers or commode deliberately obscures its function with its double-bowed and bombé outlines and lavish gilt bronze mounts of scroll and shell form. Commissioned by Louis XV for his bedchamber, it was removed by his grandson, Louis XVI, who considered it old-fashioned.* LEFT: *This magnificent mahogany high chest of drawers, made in Philadelphia about 1765, with its elaborate pierced finial, crisply carved ornament and finely cut brass drawer pulls, is a prime example of the rococo spirit as it appeared in the American colonies.*

Boucher's painting shows the comfort and intimacy typical of the age of Louis XV.

and lightness over the monumental style of Versailles. Louis XIV died in 1715 after a reign of 72 years, and there arose in Paris new types of private patrons—nobles created by the sale of offices, *nouveau riche* tax collectors, and millionaires and bankers fat on the spoils of financing 25 years of disastrous wars. They luxuriated in a new artistic freedom, indulged their highly individualistic tastes, and welcomed fresh ideas in decoration. ■ A society devoted to material comfort and pre-occupied with personal pleasure demanded constant variety, surprise, and originality. A new style emerged, called at first *rocaille* or *moderne,* and later, "rococo." It was perfectly suited to a time of experimentation and impatience with rules and restrictions not only in the arts, but in politics and the sciences as well. ■ The 17th century doctrine that decoration was subject to architecture was reversed; now decoration dictated form. A logical system of vertical and horizontal construction was masked by an ingenious use of continuous undulating curves, and a dazzling array of twisting naturalistic ornament

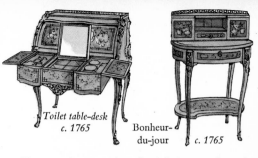

Toilet table-desk c. 1765

Bonheur-du-jour c. 1765

Marquetry in geometric or floral designs, as shown in detail below, was executed in highly colorful, exotic woods—amaranth, satinwood, tulipwood, kingwood, and many others—imported at huge expense.

Carved gilt console c. 1750

Louis XV's celebrated Bureau du Roi was begun in 1760 by Oeben and finished in 1769 by the versatile J. H. Riesener.

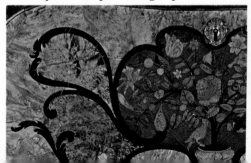

In this Meissonier design for a Portuguese palace, every element of architecture, applied decoration and furniture forms a flowing unit, the apogee of the rococo.

French writing table c. 1750

French c. 1760

German, Potsdam c. 1764

Swedish c. 17

French taste in furniture dominated all Europe. Venice produced low-cost versions imaginative in form, uninhibited in color, with painted gesso and lacquer. Ric colors appeared also in Sweden. In Germany's 300 states, French designs wer altered to suit regional preferences, except in Prussia, where Frederick the Gre demanded cabinetwork as close as possible to Parisian originals, and importe French-made pieces and French craftsmen for his palaces at Potsdam and Sans Souc

German c. 1750

Austrian fall fro desk c. 1750

Italian c. 1750

Dutch tea table c. 1750

ow to Recognize Rococo. *This ernational style had certain definite aracteristics: Lack of symmetry; restless, id movement; fanciful treatment of ms in nature—attenuated sprays and drils, pierced and jagged scallop shells, wer garlands, and flickering flames; otic motifs from the Near and Far East.*

in marquetry and metal further diverted the eye. The deliberate use of asymmetry satisfied the desires of both the patron and the artisan. To the first it represented a personal defiance of "the rules"; to the second it was a way of going "all out," of indulging in unlimited fantasy. ■ A spur to the furniture makers of France was the formation of a guild called the *Corporation des Menuisiers-Ebénistes*. Each *maître*, or master, was required to sign his pieces by branding them with his name, which was registered at a central office. The guild protected its members from outside competition, while at the same time it furnished a guarantee of excellence to the international market. Paris became the training ground for cabinetmakers from all Europe, and her master craftsmen supplied furniture to patrons throughout the civilized world. ■ In 1754 the English cabinetmaker Thomas Chippendale brought out *The Gentleman and Cabinetmaker's Director*, actually a lavish trade catalogue with engravings of his designs. A landmark in the history of furniture, it was the first extensive and reliable book published in England devoted exclusively to furniture designs. The chair has always been a good test of the cabinetmaker's skill, and in this Chippendale excelled. He produced a great variety of forms, many with latticed, intricately carved, or interlaced backs. Although the ornamentation often included seemingly contradictory elements, the total effect was one of logic and coherence. ■ Nevertheless, Chippendale's enormous and enduring reputation should not obscure the fact that he had a number of talented contemporaries, and, viewed realistically, the *Director* is chiefly important as an index of the taste of the mid-Georgians. The designs in the book were extremely eclectic; they were listed as in the "Gothic, Chinese, and Modern [or French]" taste. The style mistakenly called Chippendale did not, strictly speaking, exist. ■ The *Director* was reprinted in 1755. When the third edition appeared in 1762, the number of plates was increased from 160 to 200, of which 105 were new. Many of the "Gothic" and "Chinese" pieces were omitted, but there was no hint of the rising international enthusiasm for styles influenced by the latest archeological discoveries. ■ Chippendale's book and, to a lesser degree, the pattern plates of Lock, Darly, Ince and Mayhew, and Manwaring, had a tremendous impact on cabi-

22

"Chinese" chair

"Gothic" chair b

"French" mirror frame

Designs for astragals

In 1721, England lifted heavy im duties on mahogany. The hardnes this wood made possible the intr carving in Chippendale designs (ABO the extreme width of board allowed broken surfaces in doors and tables.

Carved mahogany
commode in French taste

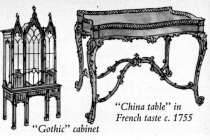

"Gothic" cabinet

"China table" in
French taste c. 1755

*Chippendale's original watercolor design,
left, for a "Toylet Table." He suggested
it be "gilt in burnished gold." Mahogany
armchair, right, with foliage decoration
and cartouches in "French" taste.*

Secretaire c. 1754

"Ribband" back settee

Breakfront c. 1754

"Chinese" bed

netmakers and patrons everywhere in the world. English designs for chairs were borrowed and sometimes transformed by craftsmen in Spain, Portugal, Italy, Germany, Holland, the Scandinavian countries, and even India and Brazil. Nowhere, however, was the English influence stronger than it was in the American colonies. ■ The rococo phase in American furniture began about 1760 and continued well into the 1790's. It was marked by a pronounced individuality of interpretation. Taste varied almost from town to town, and a good number of cabinetmakers prided themselves on the unique quality of their free interpretations of the established mode. They took the designs in English publications as mere suggestions to fire their active imaginations, and they did not hesitate to substitute local materials for the fashionable mahogany imported from Santo Domingo. In parts of New England, they might use maple; in Connecticut, cherry; in Pennsylvania,

Philadelphia craftsmen, working in the English rococo style, produced masterpieces of carving and design which equalled anything London had to offer.

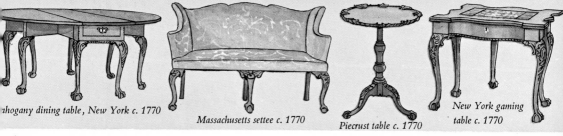

ahogany dining table, New York c. 1770

Massachusetts settee c. 1770

Piecrust table c. 1770

New York gaming table c. 1770

In America, the Chippendale style was current in the third quarter of the 18th century and diverged widely from many of the plates in the Director. As in England, rococo carved ornament was superimposed on essentially sober structural forms. Both cabriole and straight legs were used, and the ubiquitous claw-and-ball, which appears only once in Chippendale's designs and was long out of fashion in England. The highboy and lowboy, likewise discarded, reached peak development in America, as did block-front case furniture, a form found in Holland and Germany.

Philadelphia desk and bookcase c. 1760

iladelphia c. 1760

New York c. 1760

Writing table, "marlboro" legs, Philadelphia c. 1770

Massachusetts tea table c. 1760

In 1784, this print was praised as illustrating "very well just what takes place in the best homes." The medallion-back chairs contrast with the straight legs and angular tables in this typical Louis XVI salon on the very eve of the revolution.

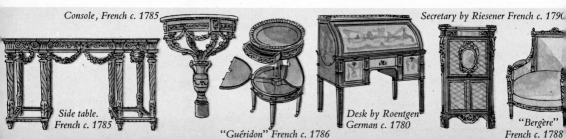

Console, French c. 1785

Side table. French c. 1785

"Guéridon" French c. 1786

Desk by Roentgen German c. 1780

Secretary by Riesener French c. 1790

"Bergère" French c. 1788

walnut. ■ The classic revival of the late 18th century came about because of two factors—the inevitable reaction against the excesses of the rococo style, and the tremendous interest in ancient architecture and decoration aroused by archeological discoveries. The excavations of Herculaneum, begun in 1738, and Pompeii, begun in 1748, caused tremendous excitement. Copiously illustrated publications espousing the classic spirit poured from the presses of France, Italy, England, and Germany, and there was a radical change in interior design. ■ When Louis XVI came to the French throne in 1774, the style which bears his name was already well established. In furniture, rococo curves were giving way to straight lines and right angles; the aim was balance and austerity. Decorations became abstract, ordered, rational. But if the forms were sober, the use of bronze ornaments, exotic woods, and lacquer was extravagant, following the taste of the Queen,

Martin Carlin, famous for his small, light, feminine pieces, designed this coffer on stand decorated with Sèvres porcelain plaques. It reflects the refined elegance and impeccable execution typical of Parisian work of the 1770's.

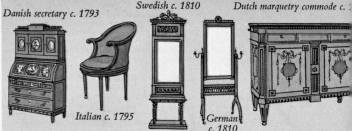

Danish secretary c. 1793

Swedish c. 1810

Dutch marquetry commode c.

Italian c. 1795

German c. 1810

This Dutch painting of 1790 shows furniture based on French and English styles, which were equally popular in the 1780's.

Marie Antoinette. In the early days of Louis XVI's reign, the court lavished huge sums of money on furniture. By the 1780's, however, a series of financial crises forced it to curtail its reckless spending. ■ Still greater simplicity and a truer understanding of classic inspiration appeared in a new vogue called *le style étrusque,* taken from paintings on Greek vases, wrongly thought to be Etruscan. The use of plain mahogany with chaste bronze mounts reflected the strong English influence that swept France after the American Revolution, foreshadowing the *Directoire* style which was to develop after the Reign of Terror. ■ In 1758 Robert Adam returned to England after four years of study in Italy to effect what he called "a kind of revolution...in the decoration of the

Adam marquetry commode c. 1775

...um lyre back c. 1775

Adam "confidante" settee c. 1775

inside, an almost total change." He and his brother James considered the earlier Palladian style as too ponderous and baroque, and eagerly promoted "greater gaiety and elegance of ornament." Their designs required complete control of the minutest details of decoration, and they created each piece of furniture for a specific spot in a specific room. By his own admission, Adam was interested in working only with "houses of consequence," and his best furniture was made for a very small group of immensely wealthy patrons. It remained for a host of followers in Adam's own time, and in the next generation, to simplify his esoteric style for popular consumption. ∎ Like Chippendale before them, George Hepplewhite and Thomas Sheraton were designers whose

Adam ornament was freely adapted from two sources: late Roman examples at Spalato, Herculaneum and Pompeii; and 16th century Renaissance. Works in Architecture, 1774.

publications, rather than their actual work, brought them enormous fame. All three, with circumstantial rather than actual evidence, have been credited with the design or manufacture of a great number of the finest surviving pieces of English furniture. But Hepplewhite apparently had only a small shop and an insignificant reputation compared to his contemporary, George Seddon, who employed 400 apprentices and carried stock valued at some £100,000. Sheraton, although trained as a cabinetmaker, had no shop at all. ∎ Hepplewhite's *Guide* went into three editions (1788, 1789, 1794) and illustrated some three hundred items "in the prevailing fashion only." Sheraton, on the other hand, consciously aimed at novelty and originality in his *Drawing Book* (1791-94) and gave technical information on construction and finishing. Although both Hepplewhite and Sheraton used Adamesque formulae and admired the prevailing Parisian taste, their "styles" differed in more ways than they resembled each other. ∎ In America, the success of the Revolution and the ratification of the Constitution brought about a change in decorative design as well as in politics. A newly independent

30

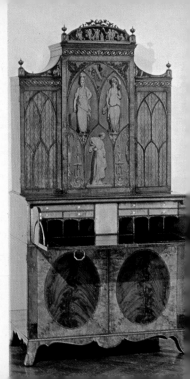

nted Hepplewhite settee c. 1790

Urn stand c. 1790

Sheraton c. 1795

Hepplewhite legs

Hepplewhite's gracefully curved designs provided practical suggestions for furniture to be used in Adam-influenced small interiors. In England, wars in America
and with France had "doubled the cost and trebled the difficulty of genteel living."
Sheraton forms, often elaborately decorated with paintings (LEFT), were more austere.

Sheraton legs

"Carlton House" desk c. 1785

Sheraton c. 1794

Sheraton c. 1794

ABOVE: *"A Lady's Cabinet Dressing Table," Plate 49 in Sheraton's
Drawing Book. He so assiduously
followed the French taste in his use
of straight lines and his fondness for
mechanical features and multi-pur-
pose furniture, that his style has
been called* Louis Seize à l'Ang-
laise.

The Federal period in American furniture is epitomized by the elegant and delicately proportioned pieces in this Baltimore drawing room. Typical of the taste for patriotic motifs applied to English forms is the cylinder-front secretary with its American eagle and shield finial. The sofa echoes Hepplewhite designs.

Wall clock

Boston c. 1800   New York sideboard c. 1782

The pattern books of Hepplewhite and Sheraton were widely circulated in America and provided models for local copies or adaptations. Thus the shield-back below is an exact copy after Hepplewhite, while the sofa above, is a New England variation of a Sheraton design. The "banjo" clock, patented in 1802, is pure American.

Sewing table c. 1796

New England c. 1800

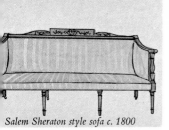

Salem Sheraton style sofa c. 1800

nation needed a national style to express its idealism, optimism, and enthusiasm. The style of the classic revival, fully developed in Europe, offered a perfect solution. Engravings illustrating the use of that style in architecture, interior design, and cabinetwork were readily available, and the designs could be adapted to suit the way of life and the purse of the average prosperous American citizen. ■ In creating the Federal style, the Americans were fully aware of the current European modes. Merchants, officials, and tourists were traveling to London and Paris; emigrant cabinetmakers from England, Scotland, and Ireland were arriving in New York, Philadelphia, and Baltimore, bringing with them knowledge of the latest fashions. Despite their great fortunes, gained in commerce and the lucrative China trade, American patrons insisted on simplicity and functionalism in their furniture. The cabinetmakers, working from established patterns, made fresh and free translations, turning out pieces marked by a kind of democratic elegance. ■ The Empire style, which originated in France, is one of the few which can be ascribed to an actual ruler. Napoleon Bonaparte owed his position to a

A tall post mahogany bed in the Sheraton style of 1795.

A fauteuil, signed G. JACOB, part of a huge suite made in 1787 for the gaming room of the St. Cloud palace.

Boldly carved classic details on this North Italian commode, c. 1790, are gilded to contrast with its brightly painted surface.

An American lady's desk follows Sheraton design, combines painted g with mahogany and restrained inlay.

Typical of French Empire furniture is this boldly impressive secretary with its lavish use of rich ormolu mounts on a stark form.

Ormolù mount

Italian Empire painted chair

Duncan Phyfe, America's most distinctive cabinetmaker, worked in many styles. This elegant mahogany and cane "Grecian sofa" belongs to his second "Empire-Regency" period, c. 1815.

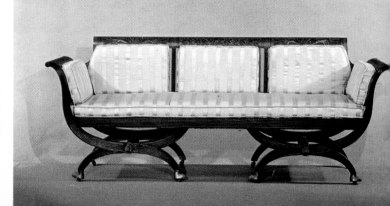

revolution and the collapse of a social system, and he was acutely conscious of the need to demonstrate the power and glory of his upstart regime. In a climate of despotism, the arts of interior design and cabinetmaking were once more used to serve the ends of political propaganda. Louis XIV had used them in the same manner, but with infinitely more taste, imagination, and money. ■ The designers and craftsmen selected by Napoleon did not lack skill; what they lacked was originality. They included Percier and Fontaine, architects and interior designers, Jacob-Desmalter, cabinetmaker, and Thomire, who worked in bronze. They aimed to produce dramatic settings of unmistakable pomp, based on the grandeur of imperial Rome. Percier and Fontaine, ignoring centuries of French tradition, imitated Greek and Roman models in furniture. Their designs were uncompromisingly severe, with large, flat areas of gleaming mahogany relieved only by symmetrically placed ormolu mounts. ■ Imperial families had replaced private patrons, who had been stripped of much of their wealth by the burden of wars and taxation.

Napoleon, surrounded by massive gilt furniture typical of his taste.

Danish c. 1810 *Italian c. 1810* *French c. 1796* *French 1804–1814*

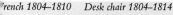

How to Recognize Neo-classic. Motifs common to all countries were: 1. Animal masks, legs and paws 2. Mythological figures 3. Motifs from Greece and Rome.

The style of the First Empire was inflexibly masculine, deliberately created for a martial society in which men of action were bent on dominating the world. Even the seductive Josephine's bedroom (RIGHT) at the redecorated Chateau de Malmaison was a theatrical version of an army tent.

French 1804–1810 *Desk chair 1804–1814* *Coiffeuse 1810* *Cradle 1811*

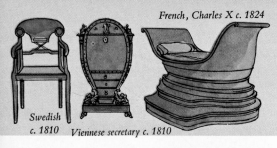

French, Charles X c. 1824

Swedish c. 1810

Viennese secretary c. 1810

In France, *Restauration* designers renounced the impersonal heaviness of an antique style associated with the Emperor. Unable to make a complete break in so short a time, they softened lines for comfort, reduced scale to suit less pretentious rooms of the period, like that shown at right.

Italian c. 1820

Charles X c. 1824

Viennese c. 1830

German c. 1820

Austrian c. 1820

German Biedermeier sofa c. 1830

French courts set up in foreign kingdoms, principalities, and duchies attempted to achieve the pomp and ostentation of Paris. Where money was available, French cabinetwork and cabinetmakers were imported; otherwise, local craftsmen, using native materials and following local taste, turned out their own variations on the prevailing style. ■ In Italy, a fondness for brilliant color and a light-hearted approach to cabinetmaking combined to produce painted furniture with more imagination and charm than the more sober French models. In Sweden, the Karl Johan style was a simplified version of Empire that used mahogany or carved and gilded wood with economy and reserve. In Germany and Austria, the widespread poverty that followed the Napoleonic wars placed limitations on cabinetwork. Greek purity replaced Roman extravagance. Outlines were straight and clean, moldings uncomplicated, surfaces almost unbroken by projections. ■ By the time of Waterloo, designers were beginning to modify the impersonal perfection of the classic style. A rapidly rising middle class was asserting itself, and insisting on the bourgeois virtues of comfort and practicality in furniture and interiors. A new style arose in France, called *Restauration* after the reigns of the Bourbons Louis XVIII and Charles X. Germany and Austria had a new style, too, labeled Biedermeier after a cartoon character who represented the prosperous man of commonplace taste. Both styles were characterized by simplicity (lines were uncomplicated by carving or applied ornament), and by warmth (woods were tawny — maple, lemon, olive, ash, pear, and cherry). ■ In England, newly unearthed antiquities and a soaring cost of living which made simplicity fashionable helped to shape the neo-classic style called Regency. The strictest interpretation of the

Rosewood teapoy c. 1820

Dressing table, George Smith c. 1808

Thomas Hope monopodium c. 1807

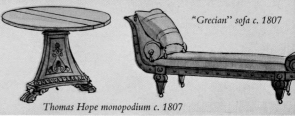

"Grecian" sofa c. 1807

In England the neo-classic style was a protest against "insolidity" and a revolt against what Walpole called "Mr. Adam's gingerbread and snippets of embroidery." Tables, chairs, couches and stools were intended to be exact copies of Greek or Roman originals, not merely familiar models with "antique" applied decoration. Highly figured wood veneers were most favored—rosewood, zebra-wood, and amboyna. Brass as well as ebony, inlay, flush with the surface, was typical.

Some Regency pieces, such as this portable desk, highly reminiscent of late Louis XVI style.

Rosewood c. 1810

Window bench c. 1809

Set of tables c. 1803

Japanned chair c. 1810

Portable desk c. 181

archeological style appeared in Thomas Hope's book of 1807, *Household Furniture and Interior Decoration,* which was based on personal observation and exhaustive study of contemporary source books. A year later, George Smith published his *Household Furniture,* an even more influential pattern book. It covered the entire range of current international taste. ■ The "Greek" or "modern" style in England resulted in pieces with two distinctive traits—mobility and practicality. They were light and portable, and often mounted on casters; many served a dual or even triple purpose. ■ In America, as early as 1805 the architect Latrobe, designer of the first furnishings ordered for the "President's House," was writing, "Greek and Roman architecture has descended from the most magnificent temples to the decoration of our meanest furniture." By the 1820's, the emotional climate was more than ever favorable to an

Circular-top furniture led to a breakdown of formality, although individual items, like the silver-inlaid monopodium above, had great sophistication. Though the antique "Greek" vogue was to last through the 1830's, this illustration shows that styles from the previous century, such as the Hepplewhite Pembroke side tables, were not discarded.

The American Empire parlor (LEFT) illustrates most of the types of furniture used in the 1830's, arranged in the formal manner characteristic of the period. In the foreground is an American adaptation of the Greek klismos chair. The massive center table rests on saber legs shod with brass claws. Other tables are supported by gilded "classic" animal paws. The two chairs at the tea table and pole screens at the window are strongly reminiscent of English designs.

identification with the forms and images of ancient republics. In 1823 the Monroe Doctrine proclaimed the New World's independence from Europe. The Greek War for Independence in 1824 fanned enthusiasm for that country's past. And the opening of the Erie Canal made the American public increasingly aware of the vast potentialities of their land. ■ Westward expansion, the factory system, and the enormous growth of mechanization led to the foundation of or extension of a number of great American fortunes. New wealth created a demand for new homes

Phyfe lyre back c. 1815

Marble top table c. 1815

Cornucopia detail, Phyfe c. 1815

fe dressing table c. 1815

Sewing table c. 1815

Stencilled sofa c. 1825–1835

and furnishings. The classic revival of the earlier Federal era, elegant and restrained, seemed too reminiscent of Europe; Americans turned to "Greek" models which seemed more appropriate to a democracy based on the limitless possibilities of the individual. This Greek Revival style was the predominant national style from the 1820's until the Civil War. ■ By the 1830's, however, international classicism began to collapse under the weight of coarse and vulgar ornament. It vanished in the 1840's, to reappear almost exactly one hundred years later.

By the 1830's, the European crossing took only weeks. Influential French and English pattern books were available shortly after publication to every ambitious American cabinetmaker.

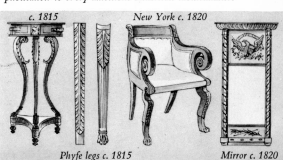

c. 1815

New York c. 1820

Phyfe legs c. 1815

Mirror c. 1820

CHRONOLOGY OF FURNITURE STYLES

BAROQUE (1650-1750). Originated in Rome, imitated in all parts of Europe and Latin America. FRANCE: Louis XIV (1643-1715). Le Brun arbiter of arts in France (1662-1690). *Régence* (1715-1723), a transition to rococo, popularizes exotic motifs (Chinese, Turkish, Indian, Persian). HOLLAND: Dutch East India Co. creates monopoly of European trade with Far East, (1602), introduces Chinese imports (lacquer, porcelain, textiles, painted wallpaper, tea) to all Europe. ENGLAND: Carolean style (1660-1685). Jacobean style (1685-1688). William and Mary (1689-1702). Queen Anne (1702-1714). Age of Walnut (1660-1714). Early Georgian (1714-1760). Style of William Kent (1730-1740). Chippendale style (1640-1755). Blockfront and shell furniture (1760's and 1770's). SPAIN: Philip V (1700-1746) introduces French vogue. GERMANY AND AUSTRIA: Native Baroque style (1680-1700). **ROCOCO (1730-1775).** FRANCE: (1730-1755). Louis XV (1715-1747). Patronage of Mme. de Pompadour dominates all decorative arts (1745-1764). *Furniture Makers:* J. F. Oeben, Pierre Migeon II, Lacroix, Sené. ENGLAND: Rococo style (1745-1765). Age of Mahogany (1714-1760). *Furniture Makers:* Manwaring, Vile and Cobb. *Publications:* Chippendale *Director* (1st ed. 1754, 2nd 1755, 3rd 1762). Edwards and Darly *New Book of Chinese Designs.* Ince and Mayhew *Universal System of Household Furniture.* AMERICA: Rococo style (1755-1775). *Furniture Makers:* Affleck, Ash, Cogswell, Elfe, Gillingham, Randolf, Savery, Townsend-Goddard family. ITALY: Painted Venetian furniture in the French taste (1750's). GERMANY: Cuvilliès introduces extreme rococo (1730's). SPAIN and PORTUGAL: Chippendale designs added to French influence. **CLASSIC REVIVAL (1750's-1790's).** *Publications:* Caylus *Receuil* showing Egyptian, Etruscan, Greek and Roman art. Winkelman's *Arts of Antiquity* made clear distinction between Greek and Roman styles. Piranesi *Diverse Maniere* introduced Egyptian taste in decoration. FRANCE: Louis XVI (1747-1793). *Furniture Makers:* Dubois, Carlin, Beneman, Saunier, Riesener, Weisweiler, Jacob. GERMANY: *Furniture Maker:* David Roentgen, most celebrated cabinetmaker of Europe. AUSTRIA: Distinctively native designs (1780-1830). SPAIN: Charles III's royal workshop copies Louis XVI and Sheraton models. ENGLAND: Late Georgian style (1760-1820). Age of Satinwood (1760's-1800). *Furniture Makers:* Thomas Chippendale and Thomas Chippendale II, working in Adam style (1760's-1779); Hallett, Hepplewhite, Linnell, Seddon, Shearer. *Publications:* R. and J. Adam *Works* 1773. Hepplewhite *Guide* 1788. Sheraton *Drawing Book* 1791-1794. AMERICA: Federal style (1790-1810). **NEO-CLASSIC (1795-1830's).** FRANCE: Directoire style (1795-1799). Bonaparte's Egyptian campaign spurs Egyptian taste in furniture. Consulat style (1799-1804). Empire style (1804-1814). Restauration (1814-1830). Louis XVIII (1814-1824). Charles X (1824-1830). ENGLAND: Regency style (1811-1820). *Publications:* Hope *Household Furniture.* Smith *Collection of Designs.* Ackermann *Repository.* Smith *Guide.* GERMANY AND AUSTRIA: Biedermeier style (1820's-1830's). ITALY: Italian Directoire and Empire style (1808-1814). AMERICA: American Empire or Greek Revival style (1820-1860). *Furniture Makers:* Duncan Phyfe. Lannuier.

INDEX

BAROQUE

English c. 1702

Spanish vargeño
17th century

French table apron 17th century

American day bed c. 1715

English cabinet 1702–1730

English wine cooler c. 17

ROCOCO

Austrian c. 1760

English "piecrust" c. 1760

American c. 1760

French clock base c. 1740

German c. 1740

Italian c. 1760

Dutch c. 1750